Minerals

by Adele D. Richardson

Consultant:
Francesca Pozzi, Research Associate
Center for International Earth Science Information Network
Columbia University

Bridgestone Books
an imprint of Capstone Press
Mankato, Minnesota

Bridgestone Books are published by Capstone Press
151 Good Counsel Drive, P.O. Box 669, Mankato, Minnesota 56002
http://www.capstone-press.com

Library of Congress Cataloging-in-Publication Data
Richardson, Adele, 1966–
    Minerals/by Adele D. Richardson.
    p. cm.—(The Bridgestone science library)
    Includes bibliographical references and index.
    ISBN 0-7368-0952-X
    1. Minerals—Juvenile literature. [1. Minerals.] I. Title. II. Series.
QE365.2 .R53 2002
549—dc21   00-012594

Summary: Discusses minerals, their properties, the different types, and their relationship
    to humans.

Editorial Credits
Erika Mikkelson, editor; Karen Risch, product planning editor; Linda Clavel, designer
    and illustrator; Jeff Anderson, photo researcher

Photo Credits
Brian Parker/TOM STACK & ASSOCIATES, 10
Capstone Press/Gary Sundermeyer, 8 (1-9)
Digital Wisdom, globe image
Joe Viesti/The Viesti Collection, Inc., 14
Mary A. Root/Root Resources, 6
Pictor, 8 (10)
T. Tracy/FPG International LLC, 18
Tom & Therisa Stack/TOM STACK & ASSOCIATES, 16
Visuals Unlimited/Mark A. Schneider, cover, 1; Steve McCutcheon, 4; Ken Lucas, 12;
    Nancy P. Alexander, 20

Cover photo: Calcite and fluorite

1 2 3 4 5 6 07 06 05 04 03 02

Table of Contents

Fun Fact

People sometimes mistake a yellow mineral called pyrite for gold. People often call pyrite "fool's gold."

What Are Minerals?

Minerals are solid substances found in nature. They are not made by plants or animals. Minerals are the most common material on Earth. They can be found on Earth's surface and underground. Minerals also have been discovered on other planets and in meteorites.

Scientists know of more than 3,000 kinds of minerals. Only about 100 of these minerals are common and easy to find. Some common minerals are silver, quartz, and copper. Halite and talc also are common. Halite is ground up and used as table salt. Talc is made into talcum powder.

Some minerals are hard to find. Scientists may spend months searching for a rare mineral. They use large machines to drill deep into Earth. Some of the rarest minerals are gems. Diamonds and black opals are some of the rarest gems. Black opals are found only in Australia.

Miners search for minerals in dirt and rock.

Properties of Minerals

Minerals have certain properties that help identify them. The properties are luster, cleavage, streak, specific gravity, and hardness.

Luster describes how shiny a mineral is. A mineral with a metallic luster is shiny. A non-metallic luster is dull.

Cleavage is the way a mineral naturally splits apart. Some minerals break into cubes. Other minerals break into unusual shapes.

Scientists identify some minerals by their streak. Scientists rub the mineral across a piece of rough, white porcelain. The colored powder left behind helps identify the mineral.

The specific gravity of a mineral refers to its weight. The weight of the mineral is compared to the weight of an equal volume of water.

The hardness of a mineral depends on how easily it can be scratched. Scientists use the Mohs scale to measure hardness.

Scientists can identify a mineral by rubbing it against a piece of porcelain.

The Mohs Scale of Hardness

1. Talc

2. Gypsum

3. Calcite

4. Fluorite

5. Apatite

6. Orthoclase

7. Quartz

8. Topaz

9. Corundum

10. Diamond

The Mohs Scale of Hardness

In 1822, scientist Friedrich Mohs invented a scale of hardness to help organize minerals. Scientists group minerals by hardness according to the Mohs scale.

The Mohs scale rates 10 minerals from 1 to 10. Each number stands for the hardness of a mineral. Talc, rated 1, is the softest. Diamond, rated 10, is the hardest.

Minerals low on the Mohs scale can be scratched by a fingernail. These soft minerals cannot scratch many other surfaces. Minerals high on the scale are difficult to scratch. A diamond can only be scratched by another diamond. Diamonds are hard enough to scratch and cut glass and metal.

Scientists compare minerals to the minerals on the scale. They scratch a mineral with the minerals on the scale. If a mineral can be scratched, it is softer than the one on the scale. Scientists can then put the mineral into the correct group.

What Is a Mineralogist?

A mineralogist is a scientist who studies minerals. Some mineralogists travel all over the world. They learn about Earth and where minerals can be found in it. Mineralogists often help find new deposits of important minerals, such as iron and diamonds.

Crystals

Most minerals are crystals. The word "crystal" comes from the Greek word "kryos." Kryos means icy cold. Many crystals look like colored ice.

Crystals form when melted rocks and minerals inside Earth cool. Small crystals form if the rocks and minerals cool quickly. The crystals are large if the rocks and minerals cool slowly over thousands of years.

Some crystals are found on top of the ground. Melted rocks and minerals may have bubbled up in springs or flowed into streams. Other crystals are found by digging deep into the earth. Miners take rocks from the ground and check them for crystals.

People use crystals in many ways. Fluorite is in toothpaste. It helps protect teeth from cavities. Sulfur is a yellow crystal found near volcanoes and hot springs. People make rubber and fertilizers from sulfur. Quartz is needed to make glass, sandpaper, clocks, and some computer parts.

Quartz is one of the most common minerals on Earth.

Fun Fact

Most gemstones form about 100 miles (160 kilometers) below Earth's surface.

Gemstones

Many minerals are gemstones. People make jewelry from gemstones. Gemstones can be cut and polished until they sparkle. Gemstones are either precious or semi-precious stones.

Diamonds, rubies, and emeralds are precious stones. These rare gemstones are more valuable than other stones. The value of a stone depends on its beauty, hardness, and rarity.

Amethyst and topaz are semi-precious stones. They are high on the Mohs scale. They also have beauty. But they are not as rare as precious stones.

The beauty of any stone depends on how it is cut and polished. Jewelers make many flat cuts on a diamond's surface to make it sparkle. Other stones such as opals are smoothed and polished until they shine.

Precious and semi-precious stones are mined in much the same way as other minerals. They may be found on Earth's surface or be dug up by miners.

Emeralds are rated 8 on the Mohs scale.

Diamonds

Diamonds are among the rarest precious stones. They are made of pure carbon. Diamonds form deep inside Earth under very high heat and pressure. Lava from volcanoes brings some diamonds near the surface.

Today, miners usually find diamonds in long, narrow masses of rock. These masses are called pipes. They go straight down into the ground. Rocks called kimberlite are inside the pipes. Some of these rocks hold diamonds.

Miners search for kimberlite by digging tunnels. Miners usually find one diamond for every 20 tons (18 metric tons) of kimberlite they search.

Diamonds are measured in metric carats. Long ago, people weighed diamonds by comparing them to seeds from carob trees. These seeds weighed one-fifth of a gram. A one-carat diamond weighs one-fifth of a gram.

Diamonds are the hardest minerals.

Metals

Metals are some of the world's most useful minerals. Gold, silver, and copper are metals. Metals are shiny minerals. People make cars, pots, and jewelry from metals.

Metals come from ores. Ores are found in rocks. Miners use drills and jackhammers to break up the rocks. They remove the ore and crush it into smaller pieces. Miners then melt the ore to create a metal.

Some pure metals such as copper are used to make objects. Copper can be made into pipes for plumbing and electrical wiring.

Many of the metals people use are alloys. An alloy is a mixture of metals. Copper and zinc are mixed to create brass. Many U.S. coins are made from an alloy of nickel and copper. Steel is an alloy of iron and several other metals. Construction workers use steel to build bridges and buildings.

Copper is a soft metal. It is rated 3 on the Mohs scale.

Gold

Gold is the most valuable metal. The world's money system is based on gold.

Gold is a durable metal. It does not rust, tarnish, or rot. Gold mined more than 5,000 years ago is still shiny today. People make rings, earrings, and other jewelry from gold. Gold is easy to work into different shapes.

Gold can be found in some streams and deep inside some areas of Earth. Some of the deepest gold mines are in Africa. Gold is mined the same way as other ores are. Miners separate the metal from rocks.

In 1848, workers building a lumber mill near Sacramento, California, found gold. The news spread quickly and started what was called the California Gold Rush. Within two years, more than 40,000 people had traveled to California to find gold. Many people did not find gold. But many gold seekers helped settle the western United States.

Most countries base their money system on gold.

Minerals and the Human Body

Minerals are found in places other than the ground. People also have minerals in their bodies. We need minerals to stay healthy. People get minerals by drinking water and eating food. We have more than 60 minerals in our bodies. Scientists believe people need 22 of these minerals to stay healthy.

Calcium is the mineral people have and need the most. People need calcium to keep bones strong and teeth healthy. The heart and blood also need calcium to stay healthy.

Many minerals work with vitamins and other minerals. Vitamin C helps the body absorb iron. Copper and iron help keep blood healthy. Magnesium works with calcium and phosphorus. Together these minerals allow muscles to move more easily.

Minerals are the most important resources on Earth. People use them every day. Minerals make our lives easier and help keep us healthy.

People need the minerals found in food and water to stay healthy.

Hands On: Salt Thaw

People who live in cold regions put the mineral halite (salt) on roads and sidewalks in winter. The salt helps melt ice. This experiment shows how salt melts ice.

What You Need

Two small bowls
Two ice cubes of the same size
One spoonful of table salt

What You Do

1. Place one ice cube in each bowl.
2. Cover one ice cube with salt.
3. Wait 5 minutes.
4. Compare the two ice cubes. Which one melted faster?

The ice cube covered with salt melted much faster. This happens because salt lowers the melting point of ice. Ice normally melts at temperatures above 32 degrees Fahrenheit (0 degrees Celsius).

Words to Know

alloy (AL-oi)—a mixture of two or more metals

carbon (KAR-buhn)—an element found in diamonds, coal, and living plants and animals

fertilizer (FUR-tuh-lize-ur)—a substance added to soil to make plants grow better

meteorite (MEE-tee-ur-rite)—a small piece of rock in the solar system that falls to Earth

ore (OR)—a metal found in rock

polish (PAHL-ish)—to rub a mineral to make it shine

specific gravity (spi-SIF-ik GRAV-uh-tee)—the weight of a mineral compared to an equal volume of water

streak (STREEK)—the color a mineral leaves when rubbed on another surface

talcum powder (TAL-kuhm POU-dur)—a fine, white powder made from talc

tarnish (TAR-nish)—to become dull or less bright

Read More

Challoner, Jack. *Rocks and Minerals.* Young Scientist Concepts and Projects. Milwaukee: Gareth Stevens, 1999.

Gallant, Roy A. *Minerals.* Kaleidoscope. Tarrytown, N.Y.: Benchmark Books, 2001.

Hunter, Rebecca. *Rocks, Minerals, and Fossils.* Discovering Science. Austin, Texas: Raintree Steck-Vaughn, 2001.

Useful Addresses

American Geological Institute
4220 King Street
Alexandria, VA 22302

Geological Survey of Canada Earth Sciences Sector
350–601 Booth Street
Ottawa, ON K1A 0E8
Canada

Internet Sites

American Federation of Mineralogical Societies: Kids Corner
http://www.amfed.org/kids.htm
San Diego Natural History Museum: Mineral Matters
http://www.sdnhm.org/kids/minerals/index.html
Virtual Museum of Québec Minerals
http://collections.ic.gc.ca/minerals

Index